Skill Builders
Phonics

by Colette Rawlins

Welcome to RBP Books' Skill Builders series. Like our Summer Bridge Activities collection, the Skill Builders series is designed to make learning both fun and rewarding.

The Skill Builders Phonics books are based on the premise that mastering language skills is essential to students' academic success. Because a fundamental factor in learning to read is a strong phonics foundation, Phonics Grade K addresses key concepts such as alphabetic awareness, phonemic relationships, and word recogntion.

A variety of fun activities introduce children to the relationship between letters and sounds, as well as letter recognition and writing. Phonics Grade K also provides additional practice with vowels, word families and chunks, and initial and ending consonants.

Learning is more effective when approached with an element of fun and enthusiasm. That's why the Skill Builders combine academically sound exercises with engaging graphics and fun themes—to make reviewing basic skills at school or home fun and effective for both you and your budding scholars.

Table of Contents

Letter Sound Chart

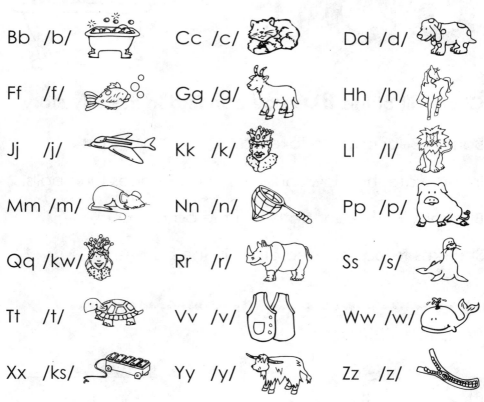

Bb /b/

Cc /c/

Dd /d/

Ff /f/

Gg /g/

Hh /h/

Jj /j/

Kk /k/

Ll /l/

Mm /m/

Nn /n/

Pp /p/

Qq /kw/

Rr /r/

Ss /s/

Tt /t/

Vv /v/

Ww /w/

Xx /ks/

Yy /y/

Zz /z/

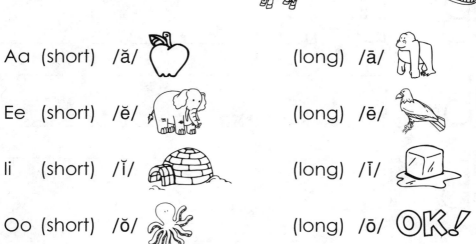

Aa (short) /ă/

(long) /ā/

Ee (short) /ĕ/

(long) /ē/

Ii (short) /ĭ/

(long) /ī/

Oo (short) /ŏ/

(long) /ō/

Uu (short) /ŭ/

(long) /ū/

Bb

Circle all of the **Bb**s you can find in the silly story.

Barney Bear loves to take baths.

In the water he blows bubbles and bounces blue balls.

But Baby Betty Bear bathes in the bathtub.

She likes to babble and crawl in the bushes.

Practice Writing

Draw a line from Barney Bear to the objects that begin with the same sound as  /b/.

Cc

Circle all of the Ccs you can find in the silly story.

Chris the cat went crazy in the candy store.

He bought candy, cake, cookies, and chocolate.

Poor Chris got a toothache from chewing the sweets.

Practice Writing

Color the pictures that have the same beginning sound as  /c/.

Dd

Circle all of the **Dd**s you can find in the silly story.

There was a dinosaur who loved to dance.

Dinah the Dancing Dinosaur was her name.

She was dynamite at the disco, and she loved to dip and twirl.

Practice Writing

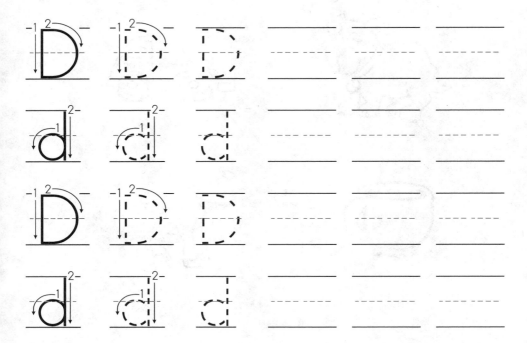

Color the pictures that have the same beginning sound as  /d/.

Ff

Circle all of the **Ff**s you can find in the silly story.

Freddie and Fannie Fish took the ferry to the fair.

They had fun feasting on frankfurters and french fries.
They rode the Ferris wheel four times.

Then, they finished the day watching fireworks.

Practice Writing

Circle the pictures that have the same beginning sound as /f/.

G g

Circle all of the **Gg**s you can find in the silly story.

The group of girls was watching the gray goat gobble grapes.

They giggled when the giraffe started gardening in the tall green grass.

Practice Writing

Draw a line from the girl to the objects that begin with the same sound as  **/g/.**

Hh

Circle all of the **Hh**s you can find in the silly story.

Harry the hound was hunting for a thief who stole hamburgers and hot dogs on Halloween.

Harry got help from Harriet the horse.

They found the thief hiding in a house in Hawaii.

Practice Writing

Color the parts of the flower that have pictures that begin with the same sound as  /h/.

J j

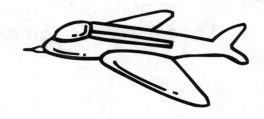

Circle all of the **Jj**s you can find in the silly story.

Jack is a juggler for the circus.

He can juggle jars of jam while jumping rope.

In January, he juggled jaguars in a jet flying to the jungle.

Practice Writing

In each box, draw a picture that has the same beginning sound as  /j/.

Kk

Circle all of the **Kk**s you can find in the silly story.

Kenny the kangaroo was in kindergarten.

He liked to kiss little kittens and fly kites.

He was kind to all the kids.

Milk was his favorite drink.

Practice Writing

Circle the pictures that have the same beginning sound as  /k/.

L l

Circle all of the **Ll**s you can find in the silly story.

Larry the lion leaped over the lizard while licking lemon and lime lollipops.

He lives along a large lake in Louisiana.

Practice Writing

Draw a line from Larry the lion to the objects that begin with the same sound as  /l/.

Mm

Circle all of the Mms you can find in the silly story.

Meatballs and macaroni is Marty the mouse's favorite meal.

Melvin the monkey is his friend.

They play Memory on Mondays and climb mountains in the middle of March.

Practice Writing

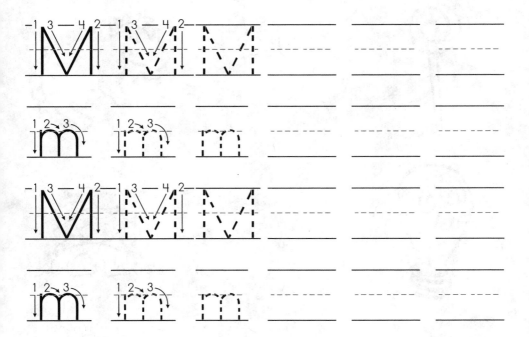

Color the kites that have pictures that begin with the same sound as  /m/.

N n

Circle all of the **Nn**s you can find in the silly story.

Nancy is a newt who lives on the planet Neptune.

She nibbles on nuts.

At night she wears a nice necklace around her neck and makes a nice noise.

Practice Writing

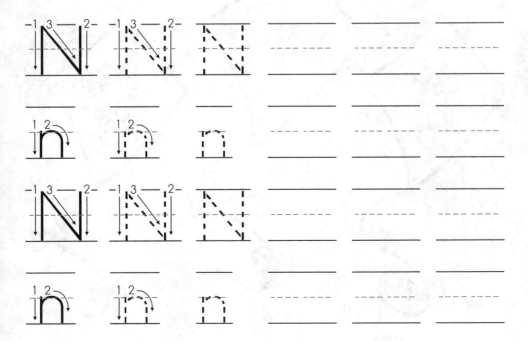

Color the pictures that have the same beginning sound as  /n/.

P p

Circle all of the Pps you can find in the silly story.

Patty Penguin plays a pink piano.

She pops popcorn on the patio and picnics with her pets, Panda and Pig.

Practice Writing

Circle the pictures that have the same beginning sound as  /p/.

Circle all of the **Qq**s you can find in the silly story.

The queen of the quail family likes everything quiet.

She said, "Quickly collect the quarters and quilts, and quit quacking please!"

Practice Writing

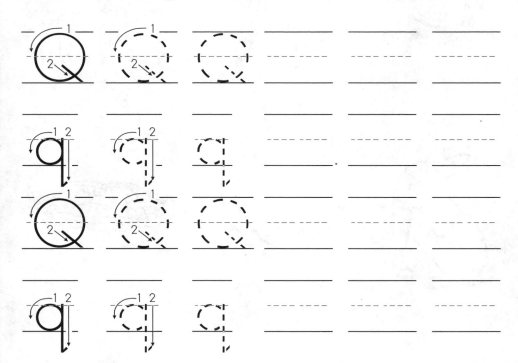

Draw a line from the quarter to the objects that begin with the same sound as  /kw/.

Phonics Grade K—RBP0008

R r

Circle all of the **Rr**s you can find in the silly story.

Rocky the rabbit likes to ride the roller coaster in the rain.

Her friend Randy the rhinoceros likes to rake the red roses under the rainbow.

Practice Writing

Color the mirrors that have reflections that begin with the same sound as  /r/.

S s

Circle all of the Ss you can find in the silly story.

Sally the seal is listening for sounds.

She hears a spider spin its web, students at school in September, and sausage sizzling in the sun.

Practice Writing

S S S ____ ____ ____

S S s ____ ____ ____

S S S ____ ____ ____

S S s ____ ____ ____

Color the pictures that have the same beginning sound as  /s/.

T t

Circle all of the **Tt**s you can find in the silly story.

Tina the turtle lives in a tent. She likes to trick and tease.

She tries to twist her tail around a teaspoon and tap dance with a tiger on the table.

Practice Writing

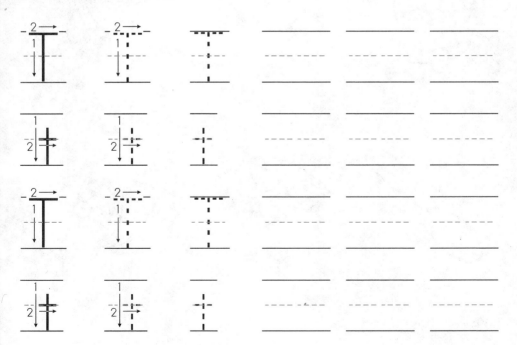

In each box, draw a picture that has the same beginning sound as  /t/.

V v

Circle all of the Vvs you can find in the silly story.

Vinnie is going on vacation for Valentine's Day.

He packs his vest and vase in his van.

He vacuums his violet rug before leaving.

Practice Writing

Draw a line from the vest to the objects that begin with the same sound as 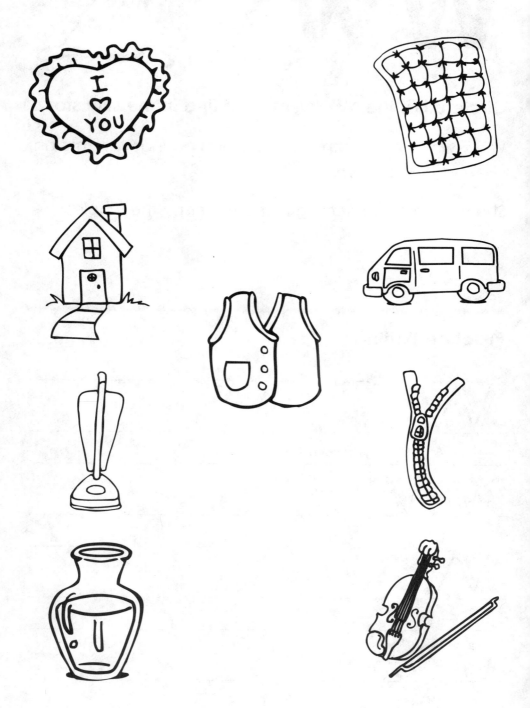 /v/.

W w

Circle all of the Ww s you can find in the silly story.

While watching out the window and eating watermelon, I saw Wendy the walrus.

She was washing her wig in the water by the whales.

Practice Writing

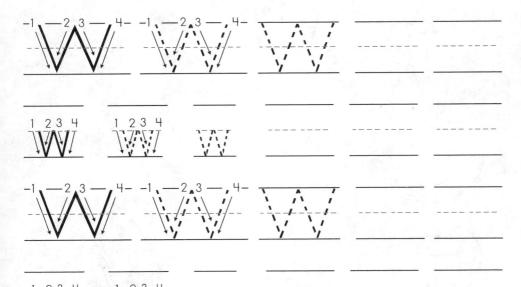

Color the pizza slices that have pictures that begin with the same sound as  /w/.

X x

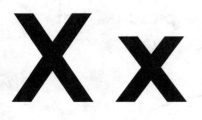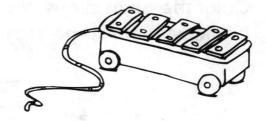

Circle all of the **Xx**s you can find in the silly story.

"Excuse me!" I exclaimed as I headed for the exit.

Xavier, my friend, is an expert at playing the xylophone.

He is excellent.

I am excited to watch him play.

Practice Writing

Color the pictures that start with the same letter or have the same beginning sound as  /ks/.

Yy

Circle all of the Yys you can find in the silly story.

Did you hear the yellow yak yodeling in the mountains?

He was yapping to his yo-yo and yelling at his yams.

Practice Writing

Color the pictures that have the same beginning sound as  /y/.

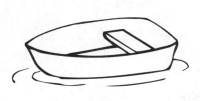

Z z

Circle all of the Zzs you can find in the silly story.

Zeke the zebra invented zippers.

He likes to hear them zig up and zag down.

He is making a zigzag zipper for the zoo so all the animals can zoom away.

Practice Writing

Z Z Z _____ _____ _____

Z Z Z _____ _____ _____

Z Z Z _____ _____ _____

Z Z Z _____ _____ _____

Circle the pictures that have the same beginning sound as 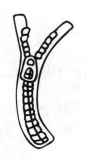 /z/.

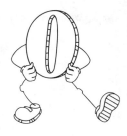

Aa

Circle all of the **Aa**s you can find in the silly story.

Annie is an ape, and she loves to eat.

Annie ate an apple on Monday, an apricot on Tuesday, and an avocado on Wednesday.

Thursday and Friday she snacked on the ants that danced in the grass.

Practice Writing

Circle the pictures that have the same beginning sound as 🍎 **/ă/.**

Circle the pictures that have the same beginning sound as 🌰 **/ā/.**

Ee

Circle all of the **Ee**s you can find in the silly story.

Emily the elephant is eleven years old.

She likes to eat eggs and to keep her ears clean.

Her best friends are Eddie the eagle and Stevie the eel.

Practice Writing

In each box, draw a picture that has the same beginning sound as /ĕ/.

In each box, draw a picture that has the same beginning sound as /ē/.

Ii

Circle all of the Ii you can find in the silly story.

Iggy the iguana got all icky when he fell into a dish of vanilla ice cream.

Poor Iggy ran inside his igloo to lick himself clean.

Practice Writing

Color the pictures that have the same beginning sound as  /ĭ/.

Color the pictures that have the same beginning sound as  /ī/.

Oo

Circle all of the Oos you can find in the silly story.

Oliver the orange octopus lives in the ocean.

He likes to collect oboes and other odd objects.

His favorites are old oars and oatmeal.

Practice Writing

© RBP Books

In each box, draw a picture that has the same beginning sound as 🐙 /ŏ/.

In each box, draw a picture that has the same beginning sound as OK! /ō/.

U u

Circle all of the Uus you can find in the silly story.

Uncle Uffens is unusual.

He wears a uniform with a unicorn on it, and he always uses an umbrella underwater.

Practice Writing

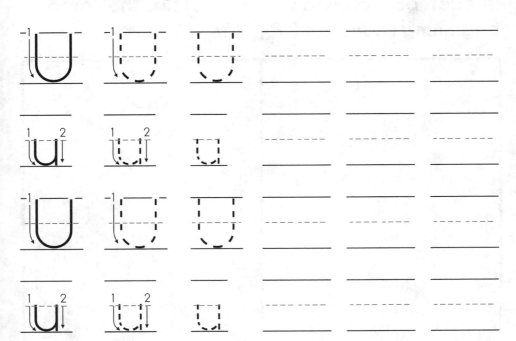

Circle the pictures that have the same beginning sound as  /ŭ/.

Circle the pictures that have the same beginning sound as /ū/.

Silly Sentences

Finish the silly sentences by circling the picture at the end that rhymes with the picture in the middle.

The green

jumped over the

The

took a ride in the

The man in the

kissed his orange

Silly Sentences

Finish the silly sentences by circling the picture at the end that rhymes with the picture in the middle.

An ugly

got stuck in the 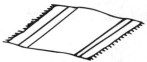  .

The cute little

lived in the red   .

A slippery

baked a chocolate   .

Phonics Grade K—RBP0008

Rhyme Time

Color the two pictures in each row that rhyme.

Rhyme Time

Color the two pictures in each row that rhyme.

Make a Match

Draw a line from the picture on the left to its opposite on the right.

Make a Match

Draw a line from the picture on the left to its opposite on the right.

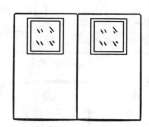

What Is Opposite?

Look at each picture in the box. Draw another picture that is its opposite.

What Is Opposite?

Look at each picture in the box. Draw another picture that is its opposite.

A Creature Feature

Look at the animal pictures. Say each name and write its beginning sound. Then practice writing the word.

____ig

____og

____at

____at

A Creature Feature

Look at the animal pictures. Say each name and write its beginning sound. Then practice writing the word.

 __oat _____

 __ouse _____

 __iger _____

 __ebra _____

Word Families

Look in the box for a beginning letter to finish the word. Write the letter on the line. Then draw a line from the word to the picture that it matches.

at

| b | c | h | m | r | s |

__at

__at

__at

Word Families

Look in the box for a beginning letter to finish the word. Write the letter on the line. Then draw a line from the word to the picture that it matches.

it

b	f	h	k	p	s

___it

___it

___it

Word Families

Look in the box for a beginning letter to finish the word. Write the letter on the line. Then draw a line from the word to the picture that it matches.

ut

| c | h | j | n | p |

__ut

__ut

__ut

Word Families

Look in the box for a beginning letter to finish the word. Write the letter on the line. Then draw a line from the word to the picture that it matches.

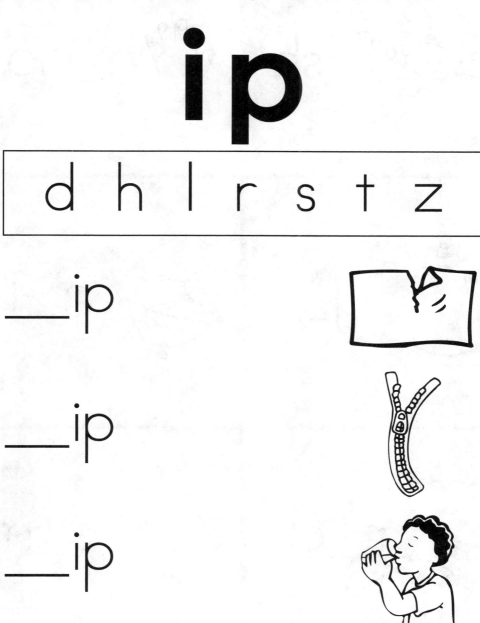

ip

| d | h | l | r | s | t | z |

___ip

___ip

___ip

Buy a Vowel

Look at each picture and the word next to it. Say the word and fill in the missing vowel sound.

f_sh

h_nd

j_r

n_t

r_ck

s_n

Buy a Vowel

Look at each picture and the word next to it. Say the word and fill in the missing vowel sound.

v_n

p_n

d_sh

w_g

r_ng

b_d

It Ends With...

Look at each picture and say its name. Write its ending sound. Practice writing the word underneath the picture.

mo_

be_

ba_

su_

ca_

nai_

It Ends With. . .

Look at each picture and say its name. Write its ending sound. Practice writing the word underneath the picture.

 bu_

_____

 ha_

_____

 cu_

_____

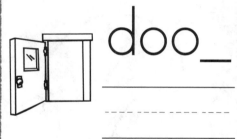 doo_

_____

 co_

_____

nu_

_____

Phonics Grade K—RBP0008

Letter Hunt

Color all the:

Bs = blue	Ds = red	Fs = green

Letter Hunt

Color all the:

Hs = green	Ks = brown	Ts = purple

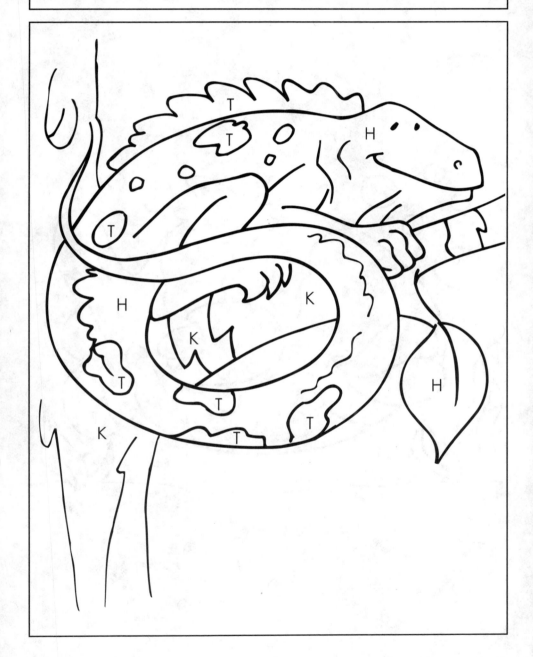

Letter Hunt

Color all the:

Ws = blue	Rs = pink	Ss = orange

Letter Hunt

Color all the:

Ls = yellow	Vs = brown	Ns = purple

Answer Pages

Page 5
lines to:

bird	ball	baby
banana	balloon	bug

Page 7
pictures colored:

cake	candy	car
cup	cow	

Page 9
pictures colored:

duck	dog	drum
doll	door	dress

Page 11
pictures circled:

fox	frog	fly
feather	fairy	feet

Page 13
lines to:

gorilla	glue	grass
grapes	glasses	

Page 15
color petals with:

house	hand
hippopotamus	

color center of flower with:
hammer
color leaf with:
hot dog

Page 17
Drawings will vary.

Page 19
pictures circled:

kangaroo	king	kite
koala	key	

Page 21
lines to:

lemon	ladder	lips
lollipop	lizard	lightbulb

Page 23
color kites with:

mushroom	mask	mouse
monkey		

Page 25
pictures colored:

nickel	nose	net
nail	necklace	

Page 27
pictures circled:

pig	penguin	penny
pencil	peas	pie

Page 29
lines drawn to:

quilt	queen	quail

Page 31
color mirrors with:

rake	rabbit	rope
rooster	rock	ring

Page 33
pictures colored:

sun	sock	snake
spider	spoon	snail

Page 35
Drawings will vary.

Answer Pages

Page 37
lines drawn to:
valentine   van   vacuum
vase   violin

Page 39
color slices with:
window   walrus
whale   wig

Page 41
pictures colored:
x-ray   xylophone
exclamation point

Page 43
pictures colored:
yarn   yak
yo-yo   yield sign

Page 45
pictures circled:
zipper   zero   zebra

Page 47
/ă/ pictures circled:
ant   ax   alligator

/ā/ pictures circled:
apron   acorn

Page 49
Drawings will vary.

Page 51
/ĭ/ pictures colored:
iguana   igloo

/ī/ pictures colored:
ice cube ice cream

Page 53
Drawings will vary.

Page 55
/ŭ/ pictures circled:
umbrella

/ū/ pictures circled:
unicorn   unicycle

Page 56
frog—dog
goat—boat
hat—cat

Page 57
bug—rug
mouse—house
snake—cake

Page 58
cat—bat
dog—log
hair—chair

Page 59
sock—rock
box—fox
jar—car

Page 60
elephant (big)—mouse (small)
sun (day)—moon (night)
happy—sad

Answer Pages

Page 61
lollipop inside of a jar (in)—lollipop
outside of a jar (out)
fire (hot)—ice (cold)
tall man (tall)—short man (short)
open door (open)—closed doors
(shut/closed)

Page 62
Drawings will vary.
  hot—cold
  on—off
  fast—slow

Page 63
Drawings will vary
  big—small
  tall—short; man—woman
  sun—moon, day—night
  happy—sad

Page 64
p pig
d dog
c cat
b bat

Page 65
g goat
m mouse
t tiger
z zebra

Page 66
b bat
c cat
h hat

Page 67
p pit
s sit
h hit

Page 68
h hut
n nut
c cut

Page 69
r rip
z zip
s sip

Page 70
i fish   a hand
a jar   u nut
o rock   u sun

Page 71
a van   a pan
i dish   i wig
i ring   e bed

Page 72
p mop   d bed
g bag   n sun
t cat   l nail

Page 73
s bus   t hat
p cup   r door
w cow   t nut

Pages 74-77
**Pictures should be colored to
match the color/letter key.**